CONTENTS

© Aladdin Books Ltd 1989

Designed and produced by
Aladdin Books Ltd
70 Old Compton Street
London W1

*First published in the
United States in 1989 by*
Gloucester Press
387 Park Avenue South
New York, NY 10016

ISBN 0-531-17180-9

Library of Congress Catalog
Card Number: 89-50446

Design Rob Hillier, Andy Wilkinson
Editor Julia Slater
Photo Research Cecilia Weston-Baker
Illustrations Ron Hayward

Printed in Belgium

PROJECT WILDLIFE

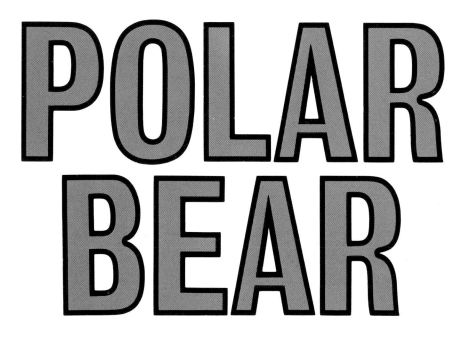

POLAR BEAR

Michael Bright

Gloucester Press
New York : London : Toronto : Sydney

Introduction

The polar bear is a living symbol of the Arctic. It is one of the most ferocious of all bears, and one of the largest land-living carnivores. The polar, or ice bear, has been known since early times. The Viking leader Erik the Red is said to have sent polar bear pelts as gifts to the rulers of Egypt. At one time, even live bears were presented to royalty. The Norwegians used the skins to line Trondheim Cathedral's altar.

Indeed, the polar bear's valued fur was nearly its downfall. When hunters were using simple techniques to kill the polar bears, extinction was never a worry. Yet by the 1950s big game hunters armed with high velocity rifles arrived in the Arctic in aircraft. They came specifically to kill polar bears. In 1961 alarmed scientists announced that only 10-20 thousand bears remained in the world. In 1965, the International Union for the Conservation of Nature and Natural Resources (IUCN) declared the polar bear "endangered" and steps were taken to ensure its survival.

Siberia

Chukchi Sea   Wrangel Island   New Siberian Islands

ALASKA

ARCTIC OCEAN

Severnaya Zemlya

Queen Elizabeth Islands

Banks I.

+
NORTH POLE

Franz Josef Land

CANADA

Victoria I.

Svalbard (NOR.

GREENLAND

Hudson Bay

Baffin Island

ICELAND

Polar bear distribution

The polar bear range spans the five million square miles of land and frozen sea that surround the North Pole. Scientists once thought the bears roamed freely across the Arctic, but we now know that distinct populations live in Alaska, Central Siberia, the Canadian Arctic Archipelago, Greenland, Svalbard and Franz Josef Land. Some bears move between areas but most stay within 120 miles of their population center. They live as far south as Labrador and Newfoundland in Canada. This is at a latitude south of London. At the other extreme, they have been seen near the North Pole.

All the bears migrate. For example, in winter the Greenland population heads south across the frozen sea between Greenland and Iceland in search of food. In the spring, they return north walking on the floating ice.

The bears get bigger as you travel counterclockwise around the North Pole. The Chukchi Sea bears are larger than the Greenland ones. The largest of all are found in Alaska.

△ A polar bear wanders across the sea ice in Hudson Bay.

Polar bear hunting

For centuries the Inuit, or Eskimos, have hunted polar bears. They fed the meat to their sled dogs. They carved the bones into kitchen utensils, made clothes and boots from the hide, and fashioned jewelry out of the teeth and claws. The hunt did no significant harm to bear populations. In 1940, for instance, only about 148 Canadian polar bears were killed.

But, in 1960, the number of deaths rose to 509 as trophy hunters began to reach the remote Arctic by airplane and joined the killing. By 1967, snowmobiles were the main means of transportation. More than 700 bears were shot that year. They were no longer seen where they had once been plentiful.

The Inuit hunters use only traditional weapons, such as hand-held harpoons, and traditional techniques such as tracking by foot or sled. The polar bear's curiosity is its downfall. When a hunter shouts and waves the bear does not run away but instead ambles closer to get a better view. Then the hunter kills it.

The demand for polar bear skins became so high that less traditional hunters began to take part in the fur trade. In Svalbard, the coal miners discovered a way to make extra money. They used "set-guns." These were traps where the polar bear took a bait, triggered a rifle, and shot itself.

Today polar bears are still killed, but killing is regulated. All hunters must obtain licenses. These are usually only issued to Inuit and others traditionally dependent on bear hunting. They can sell the pelts. A hunter may also sell his license to a non-native sports shooter as long as he remains the guide. Yet, in some areas this hunting for sport is being abused.

"Polar bears have a long association with Eskimo history. Eskimos are not considered to be true hunters until they have killed their first polar bear."

Thor Larsen, IUCN Polar Bear Specialist Group.

▽ The hunter in the photograph below has harpooned a polar bear. In some parts of the Arctic, where polar bear hunting quotas have been exceeded, poachers will raid another area and kill bears. They are after the pelts.

Trade in hides

The polar bear's coat commands a significant price in the marketplace. At fur auctions in Copenhagen, pelts have fetched between $1,000 and $4,000 each. These high prices have encouraged the illegal killing and smuggling of pelts and skulls. In Japan, individual polar bear hairs are often used to tie fishing flies. They sell for about $2.30 each.

In order to identify the furs of lawfully killed polar bears, the Inuit of the Northwest Territories of Canada are issued with a quota of tags at the start of each winter's hunting season. As soon as the hunter kills a bear, he must attach a tag to its pelt. Pelts with tags can then be sold. Those without tags are from bears which have been hunted illegally. In the United States, however, no parts of a polar bear may be imported or sold.

▽ Polar bear skins are still in demand. Some museums buy stuffed polar bears, like those with the taxidermist in the photograph below, for their exhibitions. Polar bear rugs are still bought to adorn the floors of luxury homes. And some people think it is chic to have a stuffed polar bear in the living room.

Some mammals with valuable furs are bred on fur farms. The polar bear almost joined them. In 1986, two Norwegians tried to set up a polar bear ranch on Bjarkoy Island. They planned to take the first animals from the wild to form a breeding stock of bears to be farmed for their skins. But the Norwegian government banned the project.

△ A tanner – a person who turns animal hides into leather – stands in front of some polar bear hides. Most new hides come from Greenland or the Canadian Arctic. Hunting is banned in Norway and the U.S.S.R.

Habitat destruction

The Arctic was once a remote land inhabited only by wild animals and the native peoples that lived off them. Today, the land is being invaded by others. The technological world is hungry for oil and coal. As existing supplies diminish and become more expensive, the reserves hidden below the Arctic's permanently frozen ground become increasingly attractive.

Exploring for and extracting these resources brings more people to the Arctic. In turn, more people means greater disturbance to wildlife. For example, careless workers driving snowmobiles have caused polar bear mothers to abandon their cubs. About 50 bears get killed each year in the Northwest Territories of Canada because of the people working in industry.

▽ The map shows the slow but steady invasion of the Arctic by the northern nations. More comfortable living conditions in centrally heated buildings, and ease of access in light aircraft, helicopters and snow-mobiles has meant that people can now live in the coldest and most desolate places on earth.

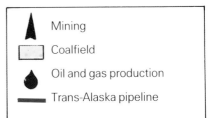

▲	Mining
▢	Coalfield
⬤	Oil and gas production
▬	Trans-Alaska pipeline

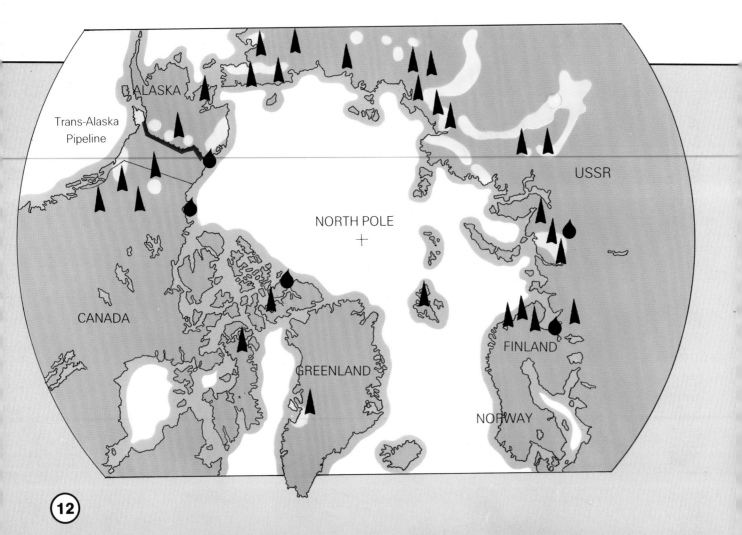

Trans-Alaska Pipeline

ALASKA

USSR

NORTH POLE +

CANADA

GREENLAND

FINLAND

NORWAY

Taking oil from the Arctic seriously threatens the polar bear. Oil spills can be very dangerous. A bear with oil on its coat cannot regulate its body temperature properly. If the bear eats the oil while grooming it could die. A large spill, like the one caused by the grounding of a tanker off Alaska in March 1989, could be disastrous. The black oil could freeze in the ice, allowing it to absorb the sun's heat and melt. This would mean the bears would no longer be able to walk out onto the ice.

Lately scientists have been learning how pollution could eventually lead to the warming of the earth's atmosphere. This could gradually melt the Arctic ice cap. The polar bear would then have less and less territory in which to live.

Polar bears are attracted to oil rigs and other installations. They can be very dangerous to oil rig workers. The workers first attempt to scare the bears away with fire crackers and gunshots. But if the bear does not go, it is shot.

▽ All across the Arctic, man and polar bear are meeting more often. The disturbance can be fatal for the bear.

Pollution

The Arctic seascape looks so pure with all the clean white snow and the crystal clear ice. But this is an illusion. Hidden in the snow are some deadly man-made poisons, some of which are blown to the Arctic in the wind. They come from the industrial complexes to the south and are deposited on the frozen sea in the north.

The pollutants find their way into the Arctic food chain. That is, they are taken up by tiny planktonic organisms floating on the sea's surface. Tiny animals, such as worms, eat the poison-containing plankton.

Fish then eat the worms. Larger animals, such as seals, eat the fish. Polar bears, at the top of the food chain, eat the seals and take in the poisons.

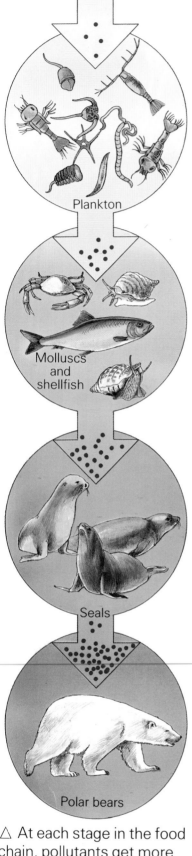

Plankton

Molluscs and shellfish

Seals

Polar bears

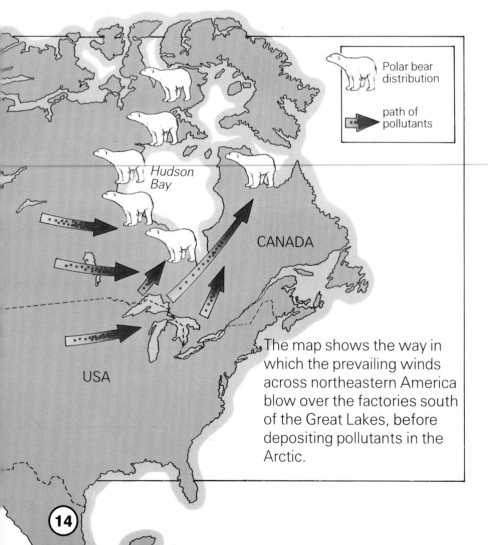

Polar bear distribution

path of pollutants

Hudson Bay

CANADA

USA

The map shows the way in which the prevailing winds across northeastern America blow over the factories south of the Great Lakes, before depositing pollutants in the Arctic.

△ At each stage in the food chain, pollutants get more concentrated. Organisms at the start of the chain, store only small amounts of poison, but those at the end, such as polar bears, contain so much it could be lethal.

Scientists know that polar bears eat poisons because they have examined bears caught by hunters. Studies have revealed a cocktail of man-made toxins in the thick layer of blubber under the bear's skin. The pollutants concentrate there in the summer when the bears are feeding and putting on fat for the winter. Scientists have discovered high levels of agricultural poisons such as DDT and dieldrin, and industrial wastes such as polychlorinated biphenyls (PCBs) and mercury. Levels are very high among bears in the eastern Canadian Arctic.

△ A dead polar bear is preserved in the ice like meat in a freezer until scavengers come to eat it. It is thousands of miles from the nearest factory or farm. Yet, was it killed by an industrial or agricultural poison? Hunters in parts of the Arctic have been warned not to eat polar bear meat. It is contaminated with toxins that are now far from the places they were made.

Behind bars

There is growing concern for polar bears kept in zoos. They all show abnormal behavior, no matter how large the enclosure. They spend their time endlessly pacing up and down, performing strange neck-twisting movements or swaying their heads to and fro. Polar bears, apparently, are only content when free to roam the Arctic.

Many zoos, therefore, aim to phase out polar bears. Nevertheless, those that remain in zoos are some insurance against any catastrophe that might happen to bears in the wild. And those breeding in captivity give some insights into the secrets of polar bear life.

"Keeping deranged polar bears for our entertainment, wherever it is, is simply unacceptable."

Bill Travers, director Zoo Check.

▽ Although it is not a thriving zoo animal, the polar bear is one of the zoo visitors' favorites.

In certain Arctic locations, such as along the shores of Hudson Bay in Canada, it is the people who are in cages while the polar bears roam free outside. The cages are mobile and are known as "tundra buggies." They look like buses with enormous rubber tires, and they can travel across the uneven terrain and through streams.

The tourists sit high above the ground where they are relatively safe from an attack by these inquisitive animals. In this way, people can experience the rare privilege of seeing in its rightful home one of the most dangerous animals in the Arctic.

▽ Polar bears, looking for an easy meal, inevitably close in on any all-terrain vehicle that ventures into their area, and inspect the tourists inside. The bears may look meek but they are actually very dangerous. Polar bears have been known to smash the windows of cars and maul the occupants.

Bears in town

People living in Churchill, Canada refer to their town as the polar bear capital of the world. Nobody there goes out after dark. Even during the day, children go to school with police guards. The problem is that Churchill is on the polar bear migration route. Each autumn the bears leave the nearby forests where they have spent the summer eating berries, and return to the freezing sea ice on Hudson Bay to hunt seals.

The bears often invade the town's garbage dump. Sometimes they come into the town itself. They can be a nuisance. Few doors will stand a blow from a polar bear's powerful paws. On one occasion, a citizen left a steak cooking on the stove and returned to find his kitchen wrecked and a polar bear making off with his dinner. Locals wear shirts with the motto "Our household pests are polar bears." But, they would not want it any other way. The bears bring tourists and tourist dollars.

∇ Churchill's garbage dump is usually the focus of polar bear activity. The local authorities, however, discourage them from staying. They could become dependent on the easy-to-find food and overstay their welcome. The dump is too near the town to be considered safe.

Churchill   Hudson Bay

The Churchill bears are not just mischievous. They can be dangerous. They have even killed several people, including one man in the town's main street. The wildlife authorities tranquilize bears that damage cars or linger at the dump. They then put the bears in a compound where they keep them until ice has formed on the bay. When they release them, the bears usually make straight for the ice.

▽ At one time, delinquent bears were captured and flown by helicopter many miles away to the north. Then they were released. However, the bears easily found their way back to Churchill, traveling up to 25 miles a day to return to the easy living at the town dump.

Protection

Polar bears have not been treated with the same consideration outside Churchill. In the 1960s, hunting caused the polar bear population to diminish so greatly that it was endangered.

In 1973, five Arctic nations – the United States, Canada, the Soviet Union, Norway, and Denmark (which governs Greenland) – met in Oslo and signed a treaty to protect the polar bear and its Arctic home. The treaty was ratified in 1976, and has been updated at five year intervals ever since. It is a model of international cooperation. It allows limited traditional hunting – a concession to the native peoples.

In both Norway and the Soviet Union hunting is banned altogether. In fact, the Soviet Union led the way in saving the species. It banned polar bear hunting in 1956 and set up the first polar bear reserve at Wrangel Island in 1960. Wrangel Island has the largest concentration of polar bears in the Arctic. Today, half of Svalbard is also a nature reserve. Disturbances like snowmobiles or dog sleds are not allowed near the area when the females are in their dens.

▷ Protected by international legislation, this polar bear mother and her twin cubs are safe from hunters.

▽ Since the Arctic is so large, it is difficult to patrol. Yet, the authorities have caught illegal traders and hunters. Recently a company was caught smuggling pelts and skulls into the United States, where the trade is illegal. In another instance, an Inuit family who had killed a female in her winter den (an illegal act) could have been sentenced to jail for 12 months and fined $1,100 by a Canadian judge. But, to keep political harmony, they got only a strict warning and their pelt was confiscated.

"Full international protection of the polar bear came only just in time. The polar bear was over-harvested and it couldn't tolerate very much more."

Thor Larsen, IUCN Polar Bear Specialist Group.

Research

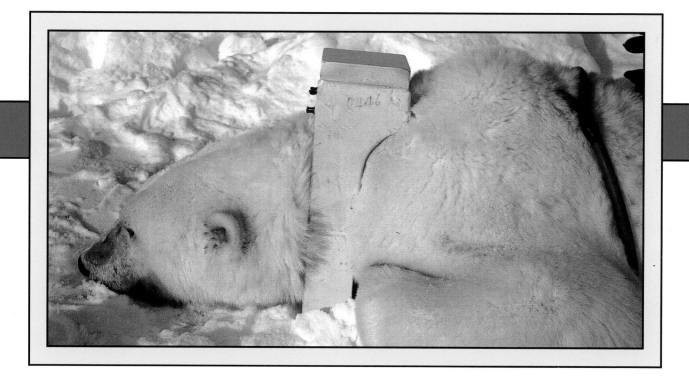

Polar bears are nomadic animals and as such are difficult to study. Tall research towers at Cape Churchill allow scientists to watch the bears returning to Hudson Bay each fall. But elsewhere they must find other methods to track the bears for considerable distances.

One method is to capture the bears and put numbers on them. That way, when researchers recapture them later they can identify the bears easily. They attach tags to the bear's ears or punch a permanent code onto its lip. When they recapture it they can find out how far it has traveled, and register any changes in weight that may have occurred during the year.

In order to capture a bear, scientists go into the Arctic Ocean in icebreaker ships or on snow-mobiles. When they encounter a bear they fire a tranquilizer dart from a special rifle. The dart puts the bear to sleep for a short time. They then measure it and put on the identification number.

△ A few bears are fitted with radio transmitters which can be picked up by satellites in space or by scientists with directional receiving aerials (below). In this way a bear can be tracked without disturbing it, and its daily wanderings discovered.

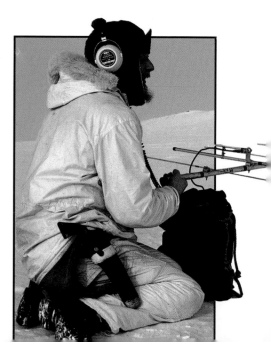

Some people consider it wrong to interfere with polar bears, since such disturbance could cause females to abandon their cubs. Furthermore, drugged bears that jump into the sea to escape could drown. However, scientists believe that tranquilizing bears is the only way to gain essential information about their life on the ice. They need facts about bear movements and population sizes, in order to introduce sensible management programs.

△ A polar bear cub has been knocked out temporarily by a tranquilizing dart and is being weighed. After the cub and its mother have been measured, researchers will watch them from a distance to check that they recover and continue their normal life. There is a.danger that human scent on the cub will cause the mother to abandon it.

The future

Polar bears are safe for the time being. Since the 1973 treaty signed in Oslo, the polar bear population has risen tremendously throughout the Arctic. Today, there are between 30,000 and 40,000 polar bears worldwide. A census of polar bears in the Soviet Union, revealed that the 5,000 bears remaining when hunting was banned in 1956 had bred successfully to build up to a population of 25,000 in 1987.

The threats to polar bears, however, have not gone away. The major danger of habitat destruction and disturbance is likely to increase as the Arctic becomes more and more accessible to industry. Related to this is the threat of global warming and the melting of the polar ice caps. Polar bears are adapted to living in a cold climate with the frozen sea on which to walk in order to find food. If the Arctic climate becomes warmer some day, the polar bear will not survive. Then there is the less visible threat of pollution in the food chain, and the danger of oil spills. Finally, there is the hunting threat — although today this only exists on a small scale.

To preserve the growing population of the world's ice bears their progress must be constantly monitored. This is being done by scientists from the five Arctic nations who meet together as the Polar Bear Specialist Group of the IUCN (International Union for Conservation of Nature and Natural Resources). It is their task to gather the information we need to know about the bears and their environment to ensure that the polar bear survives.

▷ The Arctic, despite threats to its well-being, is still a wilderness. The nomadic polar bear is still king.

4

"The polar bear is now secure. It is a good example of an animal which has been saved before it is too late."

Thor Larsen, IUCN Polar Bear Specialist Group.

Male polar bears may grow 10 feet tall and weigh over 1400 lb. Females reach seven feet and weigh 650 lb. The largest polar bears rival Kodiak bears as the largest land carnivores. The polar bear coat appears white or may be stained yellow by seal oil. In the wild they may live up to age 25.

Polar bear range

The polar bear's environment is not a stable one. The sea-ice of the Arctic Ocean is in constant motion. Consequently, a polar bear cannot retain and defend a distinct piece of territory. Instead, a bear will travel around within an area which does not usually take it more than 125 miles from its population center. It avoids other bears. Bears without cubs travel alone. They are only seen in groups at places where food is particularly abundant.

Polar bears can travel great distances. Bears migrating north against the southward drifting ice in the Greenland Sea have been known to travel 80 miles per day. When not migrating, they can average 25 miles in a day.

On flat ice, polar bears can reach 35 mph, trotting like a horse. Over uneven pack ice, they can move at 12-17 mph, ambling with their peculiar pigeon-toed gait.

Daily life

A polar bear's world is harsh and unpredictable. The sea ice may be frozen solid in cold calm weather and broken by water during storms. This affects the distribution of seals, the polar bear's primary food. So, when conditions are favorable, a bear must search constantly for its next meal. In between times, it rests, often sleeping for seven or eight hours at a time, just like a human. On warm days it spreads out with its feet in the air. On cold days or in blizzards it will curl up with its back facing the wind and sleep out the storm. It may get completely covered in snow and remain that way for several days. When the storm has passed, the bear will emerge.

Fur

To cope with the minus 58°F winter air temperatures, the body temperature of a resting bear is kept at plus 98°F. The tough hide and thick layer of insulating blubber is overlain by stiff hairs and a woolly underfur. Each hair is not white but translucent and hollow. On sunny days, it traps the sun's infrared heat.

Polar bear fact file 2

Food and feeding

A polar bear has a thick layer of fat under its skin which helps to keep the animal warm. It eats almost only meat, which has lots of fat but little fiber in it. It drinks little water, and is very lazy after eating large meals at irregular times. This behavior would seem to make them really unhealthy; but far from it, they thrive on their diet and lifestyle.

Their main food is ringed and bearded seals, the most common seals in the Arctic. Plump young seals are their favorite. One seal satisfies a polar bear for about 11 days, although it will eat a seal a day if it can catch them. It prefers the blubber, leaving the skin and muscle to scavenging Arctic foxes.

But seals are sometimes hard to find and a bear might try to catch other animals instead. For example, they might kill musk oxen or caribou. They have also been known to dive into the water to catch seabirds. Sometimes the bears may have to go without meat for up to six months. In the summer, for instance, when the ice has broken up and seals are scarce, a bear might turn to eating kelp on the seashore or mushrooms and berries in the forest.

△ Polar bears watch seal breathing holes for hours. If the bear walked about, the seal would detect the vibration. Instead it finds a recently used hole and waits. When the seal appears the bear moves like lightning, grabbing the seal and breaking its neck or biting the back of its head.

▷ The sense of smell is important to the polar bear. The smell of a kill might attract bears from some distance away. If food is abundant the bears will tolerate feeding together.

Hunting

Polar bears have many ways to catch seals. Besides waiting, they walk quietly and surprise their prey. In early spring they will crash through the snow into a female ringed seal's den and grab the pups. In late spring seals bask on the ice. A bear will stalk them slowly.

If a seal wakes the bear stops and blends into the background. Bears have even been known to cover up the black tip on their nose with a paw. At 30 feet it charges and grabs its prey. Canadian bears approach and surprise seals from under the water. Svalbard bears imitate icebergs and drift up to the prey. In addition, there is evidence to support the folk story that polar bears use blocks of ice to kill their prey.

Once they have eaten, bears wash themselves by swirling in open water or rolling in the snow. Nevertheless, the fur becomes coated in seal oil which turns the hairs yellow.

It has been estimated that the 600 bears living in the Hudson Bay area need 1000 seals per month to maintain their health during the eight winter months the bay is ice-covered.

△ This scientist is removing a non-functional tooth. He will determine the bear's age by first cutting the tooth in half and then looking at the lines of growth. Polar bears have crushing molar teeth, not sharp cutting teeth like other carnivores.

Polar bear fact file 3

Female polar bears begin to breed at four to five years of age. They will have two cubs at three year intervals. Each breeding female will only have eight cubs during her life. Females, therefore can be choosy about which male to mate with.

Courtship and mating
Polar bears convene where there are lots of seals. There are more males than females. A male will try to separate a female from the group and stay with her for a week or so. Two males may fight for a female. They confront each other with mouths open wide and showing their canine teeth. If neither retreats, they fight.

In these vicious bouts, the contestants stand on their hind legs and wrestle, biting each other and battering their bodies with their formidable paws. Sometimes they are injured. They lose teeth or receive wounds to the head or neck. The fights are rarely fatal. Females with cubs, however, stay clear of the fray. A male might attack and kill the vulnerable cubs.

Unlike adult male and non-breeding female polar bears, a pregnant female does not roam the Arctic during the winter. Instead, she digs a large den in a snowdrift. It is excavated in November on the protected side of a hill. It consists of a two-chambered cavern that will be kept at about 9°F above the air temperature outside. The den is linked to the outside world by a ventilation shaft. The chamber is always above the shaft to make sure that the warm air is kept inside. Here, in her maternity den, the female will spend the winter. The cubs are born in December. They are about the size of a rat, and born blind and helpless. The family does not hibernate, but remains active. The mother lives off her fat and the cubs suckle the fat-rich milk.

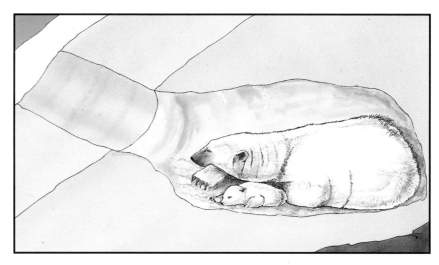

In March, the female bear will break through the snow at the entrance of her den and the family will take their first tentative steps outside. By this time the cubs are about the size of a small dog. The mother will be wary of other bears lest they kill her cubs, but will take her family to the ice for their first taste of seal. But the cubs will still suckle for up to a year.

Cubs stay with their mother for up to two years. During this time, they learn how to stalk seals.

Distressed cubs make a sound which starts as a low-pitched "snore" and develops into a high-pitched "whine." Mothers communicate with their cubs with a donkey-like braying sound. But polar bears tend to roam the Arctic in silence.

Polar bears grow fast when food is plentiful — from rat-size to man-size in a year. Their greatest test is the harsh winter, when they must scavenge food from their mother's kills. Some cubs are killed, some starve, and others succumb to cold and disease. About 70 percent of polar bear cubs do not live to their third birthday.

Index

Photographic Credits:
Cover and pages 4-5, 11, 15, 16, 19, 20, 22 and 29b: Bruce Coleman; pages 7, 8-9, 17, 23, 26, 28 and 31: Bryan and Cherry Alexander; page 10: Rex Features; page 13: Robert Harding Library; pages 18, 29t and 30: Hugh Miles/Nature Photographers; page 21: Survival Anglia.

PRINTED IN BELGIUM BY
proost
INTERNATIONAL BOOK PRODUCTION